Simple CURRY PERFECTION

The World's Top 50 Curries, With
Easy-To-Follow Instructions

BY PRIYA BATRA

healthy happy Foodie

HHF PRESS

SAN FRANCISCO

Bon Appétit

CONTENTS

CHAPTER 1
INTRODUCTION

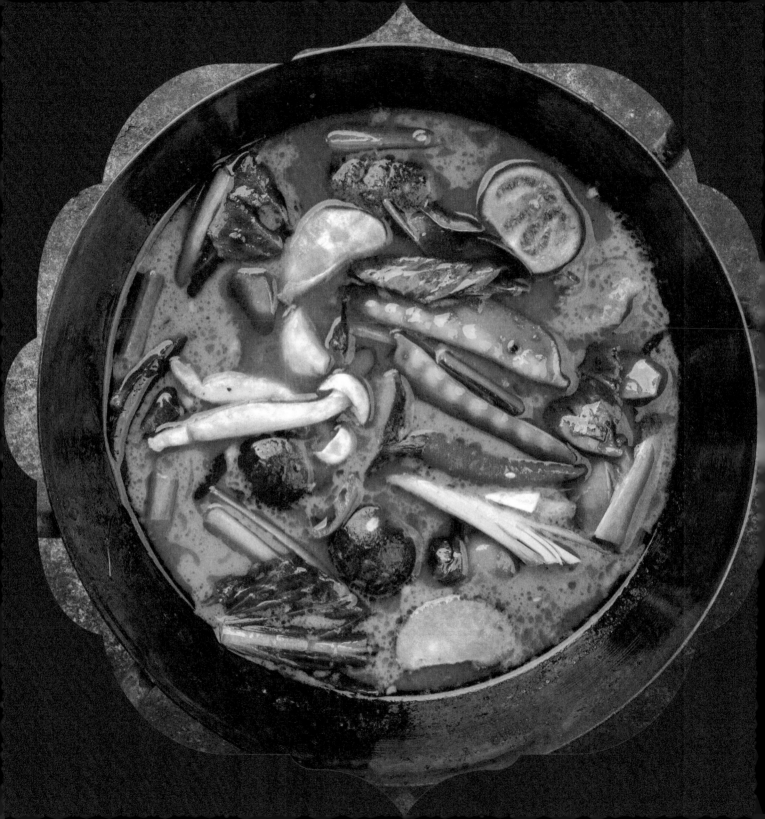

CURRY IS
FOR EVERYONE!

These innovative recipes from around the globe are sure to impress your friends and family no matter their culinary preferences! We've complied a collection of recipes for people who like their curry spicy, mild, vegetarian, or just well done with ketchup... And did we mention just how healthy these curries are?

But isn't cooking curry for experts with years of experience, you ask? With our simple and easy to follow instructions, you'll feel totally comfortable letting your kids run the kitchen. Even if they don't have any cooking experience!

So, let's get started making the most interesting and delicious curry dishes you've ever tasted. From Tikka Masala to Vindaloo, we've got recipes that are sure help you win votes from even your harshest critics. Once you start experimenting with our delicious curry recipes, we're sure you'll find these dishes are unimpeachable!

CHAPTER 2
Recipes

LENTIL CURRY

PREP TIME: 10 MINUTES | COOK TIME: 30 MINUTES | SERVINGS: 8

Ingredients

- 2 cups red lentils
- 1 tablespoon vegetable oil
- 1 yellow onion
- 3 tablespoons curry paste

- 1 tablespoon yellow curry powder
- 1 tablespoon garam masala powder
- 1 teaspoon salt

- 2 cloves garlic, finely minced
- 1 teaspoon fresh ginger, finely grated
- 1 (14 oz.) can crushed tomatoes

Directions

1. Rinse lentils and place in a pot with enough water to just cover them. Bring to a boil and reduce heat to medium and simmer until tender. You may need to add extra water to keep lentils covered.

2. In a large skillet or Dutch oven, heat the oil and add the onions. Cook for 15 minutes or until caramelized.

3. In a large bowl, combine the curry paste, curry powder, garam masala, salt, garlic, and ginger. Stir well and combine with the onions. Add the lentils and tomatoes and stir well.

PANANG CURRY

PREP TIME: 10 MINUTES | COOK TIME: 20 MINUTES | SERVINGS: 4

❋ ❋ ❋ ❋ ❋ ❋ ❋ ❋ ❋ ❋ ❋ ❋ ❋ ❋ ❋

Ingredients

- ❋ 1 lb. Chicken breast, sliced into small pieces.
- ❋ 6 tablespoons panang curry paste
- ❋ 2 tablespoons sugar
- ❋ 2 cans coconut milk
- ❋ 2 tablespoons fish sauce
- ❋ 1 teaspoon Thai chili flakes
- ❋ 2 tablespoons vegetable oil

Directions

1. In a large skillet, heat the oil over medium heat. Add the chicken and cook until nearly cooked through. Remove from pan and set aside.

2. Add the curry paste to the pan and cook until fragrant. Add the coconut milk and boil.

3. Reduce to medium heat and add the sugar, fish sauce, and chili flakes. Simmer until combined and add the chicken. If sauce is thin, reduce slightly until sauce coats the chicken. Serve with steamed rice.

POTATO AND CHICKPEA CURRY

PREP TIME: 10 MINUTES | COOK TIME: 45 MINUTES | SERVINGS: 4

Ingredients

- 1 (12 oz.) can chickpeas
- 4 russet potatoes, cubed
- 1 yellow onion, finely chopped
- 2 cloves garlic, minced

- 2 tablespoons yellow curry powder
- 2 tablespoons garam masala
- 1 teaspoon fresh ginger, grated

- 1 teaspoon salt
- 1 (12 oz.) can tomato puree
- 1/2 cup heavy cream
- 2 tablespoons vegetable oil

Directions

1. In a large pot, boil the potatoes until tender. Drain and set aside.

2. In a Dutch oven, heat the oil over medium heat and add the onion and garlic, cooking until the onions are soft.

3. Add the curry powder, garam masala, and ginger. Cook for 5 minutes and add the tomato and heavy cream. Add the chickpeas and potatoes and stir well before serving.

CURRY SQUASH SOUP

PREP TIME: 15 MINUTES | COOK TIME: 1 HOUR | SERVINGS: 6

Ingredients

- 1 large butternut squash, peeled and cubed.
- 1 yellow onion, finely chopped
- 3 large carrots, peeled and chopped
- 3 celery stalks, chopped
- 2 cloves garlic, minced
- 6 cups chicken or vegetable stock
- 1 sprig fresh thyme
- 2 tablespoons yellow curry powder
- 2 tablespoons vegetable oil

Directions

1. In a large Dutch oven, heat the oil over medium heat and add the squash, onion, carrots, and celery. Cook until they become slightly soft.

2. Add the garlic and thyme and cook an additional minute.

3. Add the stock and curry powder and simmer over medium heat until all of the vegetables are soft.

4. Pour everything into a blender and blend until smooth. Serve immediately.

COCONUT CHICKEN CURRY

PREP TIME: 20 MINUTES | COOK TIME: 45 MINUTES | SERVINGS: 6

Ingredients

- 2 lbs. Chicken breasts or thighs
- 3 tablespoons yellow curry powder
- 1/2 yellow onion, sliced
- 3 cloves garlic, finely chopped
- 1 (14 oz.) can coconut milk
- 1 (28 oz.) can peeled tomatoes, crushed
- 1 tablespoon salt
- 1 tablespoon black pepper
- 2 tablespoons vegetable oil

Directions

1. Cut chicken into chunks and season with salt and black pepper.

2. Heat oil in a Dutch oven over medium heat. Add the onions and garlic, and cook until soft. About 2 minutes.

3. Add the chicken and curry powder, and cook until the chicken is almost cooked through.

4. Add the coconut milk and tomatoes and stir well. Turn heat down to medium low and simmer for 35 minutes. Serve with steamed basmati rice.

CHANA MASALA

Ingredients

- 2 (12 oz.) cans chickpeas
- 1 yellow onion, finely chopped
- 3 cloves garlic, minced
- 1 tomato, chopped
- 1 tablespoon fresh ginger, grated
- 1 teaspoon coriander, ground
- 1 teaspoon garam masala
- 1/2 teaspoon turmeric, ground
- 1/2 teaspoon cayenne pepper
- 1 teaspoon salt
- 2 tablespoons vegetable oil
- Water

Directions

1. In a food processor, combine the onion, garlic, ginger, tomato, and cayenne pepper. Grind until it forms a paste.

2. In a skillet, heat the oil over medium heat. Stir in the onion paste and cook until browned. About 3 to 4 minutes.

3. Add the coriander, garam masala, turmeric, and salt and cook another 2 to 3 minutes.

4. Stir water into the mixture, add the chickpeas, and cook over medium heat for 10 to 15 minutes.

THAI CURRY SOUP

PREP TIME:15 MINUTES | COOK TIME: 45 MINUTES | SERVINGS: 4

Ingredients

- 1 cup medium shrimp, peeled and deveined
- 1 tablespoon vegetable oil
- 1 clove garlic, minced
- 2 tablespoons lemongrass, minced
- 1 teaspoon fresh ginger, grated
- 2 teaspoons red curry paste
- 1/4 cup cilantro, chopped
- 4 cups chicken or vegetable broth
- 2 tablespoons soy sauce
- 1 (12 oz.) can coconut milk
- 1/2 cup white mushrooms, sliced
- 2 tablespoons lime juice
- 2 tablespoons green onions, thinly sliced
- Rice noodles

Directions

1. In a large pot, heat oil over medium heat and add the garlic, lemongrass, and ginger, cooking until fragrant. Add the curry paste and stir well.

2. Add the chicken broth and soy sauce, and bring to a boil. Reduce heat to medium and allow to simmer for 20 minutes.

3. Add the coconut milk, shrimp, mushrooms, lime juice, and cilantro. Cook until shrimp are no longer translucent.

4. Bring a pot of water to a boil and add the noodles. Cook until soft, drain, and rinse with cold water. Serve with the soup.

CHICKEN TIKKA MASALA

PREP TIME: 20 MINUTES | COOK TIME: 1 HOUR | SERVINGS: 8

Ingredients

- 2 lbs. chicken breast, cubed
- 2 lbs. chicken thighs, cubed
- 1 cup plain yogurt
- 1 tablespoon garam masala
- Salt and black pepper
- 1 yellow onion, finely chopped
- 3 cloves garlic, minced
- 1 (28 oz.) can peeled tomatoes, crushed
- 1 tablespoon fresh ginger, grated
- 1/2 teaspoon ground cumin
- 1/2 teaspoon ground coriander
- 1/2 teaspoon ground cayenne pepper
- 1 cup heavy cream

Directions

1. In a large bowl, combine the yogurt, 1 teaspoon garam masala, salt, pepper, cayenne pepper, and half the coriander. Add the chicken and stir to coat. Cover and allow to marinate at least one hour and up to four hours.

2. Lay the chicken on a broiler rack and set broiler to high. Cook chicken until lightly charred on both sides. Remove and set aside.

3. In a Dutch oven, add the oil, cumin, onion and garlic. Cook 10 to 15 minutes or until onions are translucent.

4. Stir in the tomatoes and cook until tomatoes have broken down.

5. Add the remaining garam masala and coriander. Add the chicken and heavy cream. Simmer for 10 minutes and serve with steamed basmati rice.

CURRY CHICKEN SALAD

PREP TIME: 20 MINUTES | SERVINGS: 6

Ingredients

- 1 rotisserie chicken, chopped
- 1/2 cup mayonnaise
- 1/2 cup apple, chopped
- 1/2 cup celery, chopped
- 1 teaspoon yellow curry powder
- 1/4 cup red onion, finely chopped
- 1/4 teaspoon cayenne pepper
- 1/2 teaspoon paprika
- Salt and black pepper

Directions

1. In a large bowl, combine the chicken, mayo, apple, celery, curry powder, onion, cayenne pepper, paprika, salt and pepper. Stir well, cover, and place in the refrigerator for at least one hour.

VEGETABLE KORMA

PREP TIME: 30 MINUTES | COOK TIME: 30 MINUTES | SERVINGS: 4

Ingredients

- 1 yellow onion, diced
- 2 tablespoons vegetable oil
- 1 teaspoon fresh ginger, grated
- 4 cloves garlic, minced
- 2 tablespoons yellow

- curry powder
- 2 russet potatoes, cubed
- 4 carrots, chopped
- 1/2 cup tomato puree
- 1 cup fresh peas

- 1 green bell pepper, chopped
- 1 red bell pepper, chopped
- 1 cup heavy cream
- 1 tablespoon salt
- Chopped cilantro to garnish

Directions

1. In a large skillet or Dutch oven, heat the oil over medium heat and add the onion. Cook until translucent. Add the garlic, ginger, potatoes, carrots, and tomato puree and cook for 5 minutes and. Add the salt and curry powder, and cook until potatoes are soft.

2. Add the peas, peppers, and cream, and simmer an additional 10 minutes before serving. Garnish with cilantro and serve with steamed rice.

THAI BEEF CURRY

PREP TIME: 10 MINUTES | COOK TIME: 1 HOUR

Ingredients

- 2 lbs. flank steak or flap meat
- 1 teaspoon red curry paste
- 1 teaspoon red curry powder
- 3 cloves garlic, minced
- 1/3 cup rice vinegar
- 3 tablespoons fish sauce
- 2 tablespoons vegetable oil
- Salt and black pepper

Directions

1. Season the beef with salt and black pepper.

2. In a bowl, combine the curry paste, curry powder, garlic, vinegar, and fish sauce. Marinate the beef in the mixture for at least one hour and not more than two hours.

3. Heat a large cast iron pan until smoking. Cook the beef at highest heat until seared and an instant read thermometer reaches 125 degrees F. Allow to rest for ten minutes and serve with steamed rice.

EGGPLANT CURRY

PREP TIME: 15 MINUTES | COOK TIME: 45 MINUTES | SERVINGS: 4

Ingredients

- 1 eggplant
- 1/2 cup plain yogurt
- 1 jalapeno pepper, finely chopped
- 1 yellow onion, sliced
- 2 teaspoons fresh ginger, grated
- 2 cloves garlic, minced
- 1 tomato, chopped
- 2 tablespoons vegetable oil
- 1 teaspoon ground cumin
- 1-1/2 tablespoons yellow curry powder
- 2 teaspoons salt

Directions

1. Place eggplant on a baking sheet and heat oven to 450 degrees F. Bake the eggplant for 30 minutes, remove from oven, and allow to cool.

2. Heat a large saucepan over medium heat and add oil, cumin, and onion. Cook until onion is translucent.

3. Add garlic, ginger, tomato, and curry powder to the pot and stir well, then add the yogurt.

4. Peel and chop the eggplant and add it to the pot with the jalapeno pepper and salt. Continue cooking for 15 minutes before serving.

MUSSELS WITH CURRY BROTH

PREP TIME: 15 MINUTES | COOK TIME: 10 MINUTES | SERVINGS: 4

Ingredients

- 2 lbs. Fresh mussels
- 2 tablespoons olive oil
- 2 tablespoons butter
- 1/2 yellow onion, finely chopped
- 2 cloves garlic, minced
- 1-1/2 cup dry white wine
- 1 teaspoon garam masala powder
- 1 tomato, diced
- 1/4 cup cilantro
- 1 lemon, thinly sliced

Directions

1. Rinse mussels and set aside.

2. In a large saucepan, heat the olive oil over medium heat and add the onions, cooking until soft. Once the onions are soft, add the garam masala powder and cook until fragrant.

3. Add the garlic and cook until lightly browned, then add the wine. Simmer until slightly reduced and add the mussels. Cook until the mussels have all opened and add the tomatoes.

4. Add the butter and stir until melted. Garnish with cilantro and lemon slices.

PREP TIME: 30 MINUTES | COOK TIME: 4 HOURS |SERVINGS: 4

Ingredients

- 2 lbs. Lamb, cubed
- 1/4 cup vegetable oil
- 4 tablespoons ghee
- 1/4 cup rice vinegar
- 1 tablespoon tamarind concentrate

- 2 tablespoons garam masala
- 1 yellow onion, chopped
- 3 tablespoons fresh ginger, grated
- 1 tomato, chopped
- 2 teaspoons cayenne pepper

- 2 teaspoons paprika
- 1 teaspoon ground cinnamon
- 1 teaspoon cumin, ground
- 1 teaspoon mustard powder
- 1 tablespoon salt
- 1 tablespoon black pepper

Directions

1. In a large zipper lock bag, combine the lamb, vinegar, vegetable oil, salt, tamarind, and garam masala. Marinate overnight.

2. Heat oven to 450 degrees F. Place the lamb chunks on a baking sheet and bake in the oven for 15 minutes.

3. In a food processor, combine the onion, garlic, tomato, and 1/2 cup water, and blend until smooth.

4. In a bowl, combine the cayenne pepper, paprika, cinnamon, cumin, mustard, and pepper.

5. In a Dutch oven, melt the ghee and add the spice mixture, cooking until fragrant.

6. Pour remaining marinade into the Dutch oven and simmer. Add the lamb pieces and simmer until tender.

7. Remove lamb from the pot and increase heat to high until the sauce has reduced. Add lamb back to the pot and serve with steamed basmati rice.

LAMB VINDALOO

FISH CURRY WITH COCONUT

PREP TIME: 20 MINUTES | COOK TIME: 30 MINUTES | SERVINGS: 4

Ingredients

- 1-1/2 lb. cod or other firm white fish
- 1 cup coconut milk
- 1 tablespoon yellow curry powder
- 1 teaspoon ground ginger
- 4 cloves garlic, minced
- 1 yellow onion, finely chopped
- 1 tomato, chopped
- 4 tablespoons olive oil
- 1/4 teaspoon turmeric
- 1 cup water

Directions

1. In a medium skillet over medium heat, add the curry powder, ginger, and turmeric. Heat until fragrant. Add the oil and garlic and stir to combine.

2. Add the onion and cook until soft. Add half the coconut milk and half the water, and simmer for 5 to 10 minutes. Add the fish and cook until just firm.

3. Add the tomato, remaining coconut milk, and water if the mixture is too thick. Cook an additional five minutes and serve with steamed rice.

CURRY HUMMUS

PREP TIME: 10 MINUTES | SERVINGS: 4

Ingredients

- 1 can chickpeas
- 1/4 cup coconut milk
- 2 tablespoons tahini
- 1 teaspoon green curry paste
- 1 teaspoon yellow curry powder
- 1/2 teaspoon ground cumin
- 1 tablespoon lime juice
- 1/2 cup cilantro, chopped

Directions

1. In a food processor, combine all ingredients and blend until smooth. Serve with pita bread or warm naan.

SHRIMP CURRY

PREP TIME: 10 MINUTES | COOK TIME: 10 MINUTES | SERVINGS: 4

Ingredients

- 2 lbs. medium peeled shrimp
- 1 yellow onion, diced
- 1/4 cup vegetable oil
- 1 tomato, chopped
- 1/2 tablespoon fresh ginger, grated
- 2 cloves garlic, minced
- 1 teaspoon coriander, ground
- 1 teaspoon salt
- 1/2 teaspoon turmeric, ground
- 1 teaspoon garam masala
- 1/4 cup water

Directions

1. In a large skillet or Dutch oven, heat the oil over high heat. Add the onions and cook until caramelized. Add the ginger, garlic, coriander, turmeric, and salt and cook until fragrant. About 2 minutes.

2. Add the tomato, garam masala, shrimp and water, and reduce heat to medium. Cook until shrimp are no longer translucent. About 6 to 7 minutes. Serve with steamed rice.

THAI CURRY TOFU

PREP TIME: 10 MINUTES | COOK TIME: 40 MINUTES | SERVINGS: 4

Ingredients

- 1 (12 oz) package extra firm tofu, cubed
- 1 tablespoon vegetable oil
- 1 tablespoon butter
- 1 yellow onion, finely chopped
- 2 cloves garlic, minced
- 1 cup coconut milk
- 1 tablespoon yellow curry powder
- 1/4 cup cilantro, chopped
- Salt and black pepper

Directions

1. In a large skillet over medium heat, add the tofu and a pinch of salt. Cook until browned on all sides, remove from pan and set aside.

2. In the same skillet, heat the butter and add the onion and garlic, cooking until soft. Add the coconut milk, curry powder, and cilantro. Season to taste with salt and pepper.

3. Add the tofu back to the pan and stir well. Cook an additional 10 minutes and serve.

CURRY CAULIFLOWER

PREP TIME: 15 MINUTES | COOK TIME: 30 MINUTES | SERVINGS: 8

Ingredients

- 1 head cauliflower, cut into chunks and steamed
- 1 cup mayonnaise
- 1 can cream of chicken soup
- 1 tablespoon yellow curry powder
- 1/4 cup butter, melted
- 1/4 cup milk

Directions

1. Preheat oven to 375 degrees F.

2. In a large bowl, combine the mayo, milk, butter, curry powder, and soup. Mix well and add the cauliflower, turning to coat. Place cauliflower in a baking dish and bake for 30 minutes. Remove from oven and serve while warm.

BRAISED SHORT RIB CURRY

PREP TIME: 15 MINUTES | COOK TIME: 4 HOURS | SERVINGS: 4

Ingredients

- 2 lbs. beef short rib
- 2 cups chicken or vegetable stock
- 1 teaspoon garam masala
- 1 yellow onion, finely chopped
- 4 cloves garlic, minced
- 1 tablespoon red curry paste
- 1 cup coconut milk
- 2 teaspoons fish sauce
- 1/2 teaspoon ground
- cayenne pepper
- 2 tablespoons tomato paste
- Salt and black pepper
- 1/4 cup green onions, chopped
- 1 bay leaf

Directions

1. Season the short ribs with salt, pepper, cayenne pepper, and garam masala. Place on a baking sheet and drizzle with vegetable oil. Heat oven to 400 degrees F and bake for 15 to 20 minutes.

2. In a large pot, heat vegetable oil and combine the onion, and tomato paste. Cook until the onion is translucent and add the curry paste, cooking until fragrant. Add the garlic and cook until lightly browned.

3. Add the chicken stock, coconut milk, fish sauce, and bay leaf, and simmer for 10 minutes.

4. Add the short ribs to the liquid and place in a 300-degree oven until the ribs are fork tender. About 3 hours.

5. Remove ribs from liquid and set aside. Bring the liquid to a boil and reduce slightly. Add the ribs back to the sauce and turn to coat.

BEEF AND GREEN BEAN CURRY

PREP TIME: 15 MINUTES | COOK TIME: 30 MINUTES | SERVINGS: 4

Ingredients

- 2 lbs. sirloin or flank steak, cut into strips
- 2 tablespoons garam masala
- 2 lbs. green beans, trimmed
- 2 tablespoons vegetable oil
- 1/3 cup plain yogurt
- 1/2 teaspoon cayenne pepper
- 1/2 red onion, sliced
- 3 cloves garlic, minced
- 2 tablespoons lime juice
- Salt and black pepper

Directions

1. In a large bowl, combine the yogurt, garam masala, garlic, cayenne pepper, and beef. Stir well and set aside.

2. In a large skillet, heat the oil over high heat and add the onions and green beans. Cook until onions are soft and green beans are seared. Remove from pan.

3. Add the beef to the pan and cook for 4 minutes. Add the green bean mixture to the pan and toss well. Remove from heat and serve immediately.

CURRIED CRAB CAKES

PREP TIME: 20 MINUTES | COOK TIME: 15 MINUTES | SERVINGS: 6

Ingredients

- 1 lb. lump crab meat
- 1/2 cup mayonnaise
- 1/2 green bell pepper, diced
- 1/2 red bell pepper, diced
- 1 tablespoon yellow curry powder
- 1/2 cup breadcrumbs
- 1 egg, beaten
- 1 tablespoon dijon mustard
- 1/2 teaspoon cayenne pepper
- Salt and black pepper
- 4 tablespoons vegetable oil

Directions

1. In a large bowl, combine the crab, mayo, bell peppers, curry powder, breadcrumbs, egg, mustard, and cayenne pepper. Mix well until combined.

2. In a large skillet, heat the oil over medium heat. Form the crab mixture into six equal patties about an inch thick. Season the cakes with salt and pepper and place in the skillet.

3. Cook the cakes for about 6 to 8 minutes per side or until golden brown. Remove from heat and place on paper towels. Sprinkle with salt and serve immediately.

KABOCHA

PREP TIME: 15 MINUTES | COOK TIME: 25 MINUTES | SERVINGS: 6

Ingredients

- 3 cups kabocha, cubed
- 1 yellow onion, chopped
- 1 cup coconut milk
- 2 teaspoons fresh ginger, grated
- 2 teaspoons yellow curry powder
- 1 tablespoon fish sauce
- 1/2 teaspoon sugar
- 1 tablespoon vegetable oil

Directions

1. In a large skillet or Dutch oven, heat the oil over medium heat and add the kabocha and onion, cooking until the onion is soft.

2. Add the coconut milk, ginger, fish sauce, and curry powder. Stir well and simmer an additional 10 minutes. Remove from heat and add the sugar. Stir until dissolved.

PINEAPPLE CHICKEN CURRY

PREP TIME: 20 MINUTES | COOK TIME: 40 MINUTES | SERVINGS: 6

Ingredients

- 1-1/2 lbs. chicken breast, cut into strips
- 3 cups coconut milk
- 3 tablespoons red curry paste
- 3 tablespoons sugar
- 1/2 red bell pepper, chopped
- 3 tablespoons yellow onion, chopped
- 1 cup pineapple, chopped
- 2 tablespoons fish sauce
- Steamed rice, for serving

Directions

1. In a medium saucepan or wok, combine the curry paste and 1 cup of coconut milk. Bring to medium heat, stirring constantly. Add the remaining coconut milk, chicken, fish sauce, and sugar. Simmer for 15 minutes.

2. Add the onion and peppers to the pan and cook an additional 15 minutes. Remove from heat, add pineapple and serve with steamed rice.

FRIED CURRY POTATOES

PREP TIME: 10 MINUTES | COOK TIME: 25 MINUTES | SERVINGS: 4

Ingredients

- 2 russet potatoes, peeled and cut into chunks
- 1/4 cup vegetable or peanut oil
- 1 teaspoon ground cumin
- 1 teaspoon ground coriander
- 1/2 teaspoon paprika
- 1/4 teaspoon turmeric
- 1 teaspoon salt
- 1/2 teaspoon black pepper

Directions

1. Boil a large pot of water and add the potatoes. Cook until the potatoes are nearly fork tender.

2. In a small bowl, combine the cumin, coriander, paprika, turmeric, salt, and pepper.

3. Drain the potatoes and heat a large skillet with the oil. Add the potatoes to the skillet and add the spice mix. Stir to coat with spices. Cook until potatoes are tender.

PREP TIME: 10 MINUTES | COOK TIME: 15 MINUTES | SERVINGS: 4

✿ ✿ ✿ ✿ ✿ ✿ ✿ ✿ ✿ ✿ ✿ ✿ ✿ ✿ ✿ ✿ ✿ ✿ ✿

Ingredients

- 1-1/2 lbs. chicken breast tenders, trimmed
- 2 cups plain yogurt
- 2 tablespoons yellow curry powder
- 2 tablespoons garam masala
- 1/4 teaspoon cayenne pepper
- Salt and black pepper
- Bamboo skewers

Directions

1. In a large bowl, combine the yogurt, garam masala, curry powder, and cayenne pepper. Stir well and add the chicken. Allow to marinate at least one hour.

2. Light a grill or heat a grill pan to highest heat possible. Remove the chicken from the marinade and season with salt and pepper. Place one chicken tender on each skewer and place on the grill, cooking three minutes per side. Remove from grill and serve immediately.

YOGURT MARINATED CURRY CHICKEN SKEWERS

CURRY CHICKEN MEATBALLS

PREP TIME: 10 MINUTES | COOK TIME: 15 MINUTES | SERVINGS: 6

Ingredients

- 1 lb. ground chicken
- 1/2 cup breadcrumbs
- 1/2 yellow onion, finely chopped
- 2 tablespoons tomato paste
- 1 tablespoon yellow curry powder
- 1 egg, beaten
- 1/3 cup vegetable oil

Directions

1. In a large bowl, combine the chicken, breadcrumbs, onion, tomato paste, curry powder, and egg. Stir well and form into small balls.

2. Heat the oil in a large skillet over medium high heat. Add the meatballs, cooking until browned on all sides, and an instant read thermometer reads 150 degrees F. Remove from pan and drain on paper towels before serving.

BUTTER CHICKEN

PREP TIME: 25 MINUTES | COOK TIME: 45 MINUTES | SERVINGS: 4

Ingredients

- 2 lbs. chicken breast or thighs, cut into chunks
- 1/2 cup plain yogurt
- 1 1/2 tablespoons tandoori masala powder
- 2 teaspoons garam masala powder
- 1/2 yellow onion, finely chopped
- 1 tablespoon fresh ginger, grated
- 2 cloves garlic, minced
- 1 cup tomato sauce
- 1 cup heavy cream
- 2 tablespoons ghee
- 4 tablespoons vegetable oil
- Salt and black pepper

Directions

1. In a bowl, combine the yogurt and tandoori masala powder. Add the chicken, cover, and refrigerate for at least 1 hour.

2. In a food processor, puree the onion, ginger, and garlic.

3. In a Dutch oven, heat the oil over medium-high heat. Add the chicken and cook until browned. Remove chicken from pot and set aside. Add the onion paste and garam masala to the pot and cook until fragrant. Add the tomato sauce and simmer for 5 minutes. Add the ghee and place the chicken back in the pot. Cover and simmer another 15 minutes or until the chicken is cooked through. Serve with steamed rice.

GREEN CURRY WITH CHICKEN

PREP TIME: 15 MINUTES | COOK TIME: 45 MINUTES | SERVINGS: 4

Ingredients

- 1 lb. chicken breast of thighs, cubed
- 2 tablespoons vegetable oil
- 2 tablespoons green curry paste
- 2 cloves garlic, minced
- 1 teaspoon fresh ginger, grated
- 2 cups coconut milk
- 1-1/2 tablespoons fish sauce
- 2 tablespoons soy sauce
- 2 tablespoons green onions, chopped
- 1/2 cup cilantro, chopped

Directions

1. In a Dutch oven, heat the oil and add the chicken and 1 tablespoon soy sauce. Cook until the chicken is nearly cooked through. Remove chicken from the pot and set aside.

2. Add the curry paste to the pot and cook until fragrant. Add the green onions, garlic, and ginger and cook for 2 to 3 minutes. Add the chicken to the pot with the coconut milk, remaining soy sauce, and fish sauce. Simmer for an additional 25 minutes. Serve with steamed rice and garnish with cilantro.

THAI PORK CURRY

PREP TIME: 15 MINUTES | COOK TIME: 20 MINUTES | SERVINGS: 4

Ingredients

- 1-1/2 lb. pork tenderloin, cut into strips
- 1 can coconut milk
- 1 tablespoon red curry paste
- 1 teaspoon yellow curry powder
- 1 red bell pepper, sliced
- 2 tablespoons vegetable oil
- Salt and black pepper

Directions

1. In a large skillet, heat the oil over medium heat. Season the pork with salt and pepper and add to the pan. Cook until browned and add the red pepper. Cook until pepper has softened slightly and add the coconut milk, curry paste, and curry powder. Simmer until the curry paste has dissolved into the coconut milk.

2. Remove from heat and serve with steamed rice.

COCONUT CARROT SOUP

PREP TIME: 15 MINUTES | COOK TIME: 45 MINUTES | SERVINGS: 4

Ingredients

- 1 lb. carrots, chopped
- 1/2 yellow onion, finely chopped
- 1 can coconut milk
- 1/2 teaspoon fresh ginger, grated
- 1 cup chicken stock
- 1 teaspoon yellow curry powder
- Salt and black pepper

Directions

1. Preheat oven to 400 degrees F, and place the carrots and onions on a baking sheet. Bake for 30 minutes.

2. Once onions and carrots are cooked, place in a pot with the coconut milk, ginger, curry powder, and chicken stock. Simmer over medium heat for 10 minutes and transfer to a blender. Blend until smooth and season with salt and pepper to taste.

CURRY CRUSTED SALMON STEAKS

PREP TIME: 30 MINUTES | COOK TIME: 30 MINUTES | SERVINGS: 2

Ingredients

- 2 center cut salmon steaks
- 2 tablespoons vegetable oil
- 1 shallot, minced
- 1 clove garlic, minced
- 1 tablespoon yellow curry powder
- 1/3 cup brandy or whiskey
- 2 tablespoons butter
- Salt and black pepper

Directions

1. Rub the salmon steaks generously with curry powder, salt, and pepper. Allow to sit at room temperature for 30 minutes.

2. In a large skillet, heat the oil over medium-high heat. Preheat oven to 350 degrees F.

3. Add the salmon to the pan and sear for 5 minutes per side. When salmon is seared place in the oven until an instant read thermometer reads 135 degrees F. Remove from oven and allow salmon to rest for 10 minutes.

4. Place the pan back on medium heat and add the shallots and garlic. Cook for one minute, then add the brandy and cook until alcohol has cooked off. Add the butter and stir well. Place the salmon back in the pan to coat with sauce or serve the sauce on the side.

FRIED CURRY CALAMARI

PREP TIME: 20 MINUTES | COOK TIME: 15 MINUTES | SERVINGS: 4

Ingredients

- 2 lbs. calamari, cut into rings
- 1 cup all purpose flour
- 1/4 cup cornstarch
- 2 egg whites

- 2 tablespoons yellow curry powder
- 1 teaspoon ground cumin
- 1 teaspoon ground coriander
- 1/2 teaspoon onion powder

- 1/2 teaspoon garlic powder
- 1 teaspoon salt
- 1/2 teaspoon black pepper
- 4 cups vegetable or peanut oil

Directions

1. In a large bowl, combine the flour, cornstarch, curry powder, cumin, coriander, onion powder, garlic powder, salt, and pepper. Mix well.

2. In a medium pot, heat the oil to 350 degrees F. Soak the calamari in the egg white, and dredge in the seasoned flour. Place the calamari in the oil and fry until golden brown. Remove from oil and immediately sprinkle with salt before serving.

CURRY DEVILED EGGS

PREP TIME: 25 MINUTES | COOK TIME: 20 MINUTES | SERVINGS: 12

Ingredients

- 12 eggs, hard boiled
- 1/4 cup mayonnaise
- 3 tablespoons Dijon mustard
- 1 teaspoon yellow curry powder
- 1/2 teaspoon ground coriander
- 1 teaspoon shallot, minced
- 1/2 teaspoon salt
- 1/4 teaspoon black pepper
- 1/4 teaspoon turmeric
- 1/4 teaspoon paprika

Directions

1. Slice eggs and separate the whites and yolks. Place yolks in a bowl and add the mayo, mustard, curry powder, coriander, shallot, salt, pepper, and turmeric. Mix until combined and place in refrigerator for 1 hour.

2. Arrange the egg whites on a large plate and pipe the yolk mixture into the whites. Sprinkle with paprika and serve.

THAI CURRY NOODLES

PREP TIME: 20 MINUTES | COOK TIME: 10 MINUTES | SERVINGS: 6

Ingredients

- 8 oz. wide rice noodles
- 1 large carrot,
  cut into matchsticks
- 1 tablespoon vegetable oil
- 2 cloves garlic

- 2 tablespoons fresh garlic, grated
- 4 cups water
- 1/4 cup roasted
  peanuts, chopped

- 3 tablespoons green
  onions, sliced
- 1/4 cup cilantro, roughly chopped

Directions

1. In a medium saucepan over medium heat, heat the oil. Add the garlic, and cook for
   1 minute.

2. Add the water and ginger to the saucepan and bring to a boil. Reduce to a simmer, add
   the carrot, and cook for 5 minutes.

3. Add the noodles to the broth and bring to a boil. Top with green onions, cilantro,
   and peanuts.

TOMATO CURRY SOUP

PREP TIME: 20 MINUTES | COOK TIME: 45 MINUTES | SERVINGS: 4

Ingredients

- 1 (28 oz.) can peeled plum tomatoes, crushed
- 1 yellow onion, chopped
- 2 cloves garlic, minced
- 1 cup chicken or vegetable stock
- 1 teaspoon yellow curry powder
- 1/4 cup olive oil
- 2 tablespoons butter
- 2 stalks celery, chopped
- Salt and black pepper

Directions

1. Preheat oven to 400 degrees F. Place tomatoes in a single layer on an oven safe baking dish and drizzle with oil. Sprinkle with salt and pepper and bake for 15 minutes.

2. In a large saucepan, melt the butter and add the carrot, celery, onion, and garlic. Cook for 10 minutes.

3. Add the tomatoes to the carrot mixture and stir in the broth. Simmer on medium heat until the vegetables are soft. Transfer to a blender and blend until smooth.

KaLe aND QUINOa CURRY

PREP TIME: 10 MINUTES | COOK TIME: 30 MINUTES | SERVINGS: 4

Ingredients

- 1 cup quinoa, rinsed
- 3 tablespoons olive oil
- 2 cups curly kale, chopped
- 1 red onion, sliced
- 1 tablespoon yellow curry powder
- 1/2 teaspoon ground cumin
- 2 cups chicken or vegetable stock
- 1 tablespoon lime juice
- 1/2 cup cilantro, chopped
- Salt and black pepper

Directions

1. In a large saucepan over medium heat, add the oil, and onion, and salt and pepper, cooking until onion is soft. Add the curry powder and cumin and cook until fragrant.

2. Add the quinoa and cook until fragrant. Add the broth and bring to a boil for 9 minutes. Add the kale and cook until wilted. Remove from heat and add the lime juice. Serve with cilantro.

PREP TIME: 15 MINUTES | COOK TIME: 35 MINUTES | SERVINGS: 4

Ingredients

- 2 duck breasts
- 1 can coconut milk
- 1 tablespoon yellow curry powder
- 1 tablespoon garam masala powder
- 1/2 yellow onion, finely chopped
- 1 clove garlic, minced
- 2 tablespoons vegetable oil
- Salt and black pepper

Directions

1. Preheat oven to 375 degrees F. Score the fat side of the duck breasts with a sharp knife and lay the breasts fat side down in a cold pan. Set the heat for medium high and cook for approximately 10 to 15 minutes, or until most of the fat has rendered.

2. Flip the duck and place the pan in the oven and continue cooking.

3. In a medium saucepan over medium heat, heat the oil and add the onion, cooking until soft. Add the garlic and cook 1 additional minute. Add the coconut milk and curry powder and bring to a boil. Reduce heat and simmer until thickened.

4. Remove duck breast from oven once an instant read thermometer reads 130 degrees F. Allow to rest 10 minutes. Slice duck breast against the grain and drizzle with coconut curry sauce to serve.

CURRY DUCK BREAST

COCONUT SHRIMP NOODLES

PREP TIME: 10 MINUTES | COOK TIME: 10 MINUTES | SERVINGS: 4

Ingredients

- 2 tablespoons vegetable oil
- 1 shallot, finely chopped
- 1 package rice noodles
- 2 cloves garlic, minced
- 2 tablespoons yellow curry paste
- 1 can coconut milk
- 12 shrimp, peeled
- 2 cups fresh spinach
- 1 tablespoon fish sauce
- Salt
- 1/3 cup cilantro

Directions

1. Soak the noodles in warm water for 10 minutes.

2. In a large saucepan or Dutch oven, heat the oil and add the shallot, cooking until softened. Add the garlic, and curry paste and cook until fragrant. Add the coconut milk, and simmer for 5 minutes.

3. Stir in the shrimp and spinach and cook until the shrimp are opaque. Remove from heat and add the noodles and fish sauce. Season to taste with salt and top with cilantro.

GREEN CURRY SHRIMP

PREP TIME: 30 MINUTES | COOK TIME: 20 MINUTES | SERVINGS: 4

Ingredients

- 1 lb. medium shrimp, peeled
- 1 can coconut milk
- 2 tablespoons green curry paste
- Juice from 2 limes
- 1 tablespoon soy sauce
- 2 tablespoons vegetable oil
- 1/2 lb. green beans

Directions

1. In a large skillet, heat the oil over medium high heat and add the green beans. Add the green curry paste and coconut milk and boil. Reduce heat and simmer for 6 to 8 minutes.

2. Add the shrimp. Cook until the shrimp are opaque. Remove shrimp from sauce and simmer to thicken. Serve shrimp with steamed rice.

LAMB BIRYANI

PREP TIME: 30 MINUTES | COOK TIME: 1 HOUR | SERVINGS: 8

Ingredients

- 1 lb. lamb, cubed
- 2-1/2 cups basmati rice
- 4 tablespoons vegetable oil
- 6 cloves
- 4 cardamom pods

- 4 cinnamon sticks
- 3 yellow onions
- 2 cloves garlic, minced
- 1 tablespoon fresh ginger, grated
- 3 tomatoes, diced

- 2 teaspoons paprika
- 4 tablespoons plain yogurt
- 2 tablespoons lemon juice
- 2 teaspoons salt
- 7-1/2 cups water

Directions

1. In a Dutch oven, heat the oil and add the cloves, cardamom, and cinnamon, cooking until fragrant. Add the onions and cook 5 minutes. Add the garlic and ginger and cook one additional minute.

2. Season the lamb with salt and pepper and add to the pot. Cook about 15 minutes.

3. Add the tomatoes and paprika, and stir well. Add the yogurt and lemon juice and continue cooking until the lamb is fork tender.

4. In another saucepan, bring the water to a boil and add the rice. Cook until the rice is nearly finished but still al dente. Drain.

5. In a large pot layer the rice and lamb mixture. Cover the pot and cook another 15 minutes or until the rice is tender.

MALAYSIAN CHICKEN THIGHS

PREP TIME: 20 MINUTES | COOK TIME: 45 MINUTES | SERVINGS: 8

Ingredients

- 8 chicken thighs
- 3 tablespoons vegetable oil
- 4 cloves garlic
- 1 tablespoon fresh ginger, grated

- 1-1/2 tablespoon red curry paste
- 2 teaspoons garam masala
- 1 can coconut milk
- 1 teaspoon Chinese five spice

- 1 tablespoon fish sauce
- 1 teaspoon cayenne pepper
- 1/3 cup green onions

Directions

1. In a food processor, combine the green onions, ginger, and garlic. Blend until smooth.

2. In a large skillet over medium heat, add the oil and cook the chicken until well browned. Set aside.

3. Add the onion puree to the skillet and cook until fragrant. Add the cayenne pepper, curry paste, garam masala, and five spice, and cook for 2 minutes. Add the coconut milk and fish sauce and stir and simmer until combined.

4. Place the chicken back in the skillet and simmer for 20 minutes.

GRILLED CURRY CHICKEN WINGS

PREP TIME: 40 MINUTES | COOK TIME: 10 MINUTES | SERVINGS: 3

Ingredients

- 2 lbs. Chicken wings
- 1/2 cup plain yogurt
- 2 tablespoons yellow curry powder
- 1/4 teaspoon cayenne pepper
- 1 tablespoon vegetable oil
- Salt and black pepper

Directions

1. In a large bowl, combine the yogurt, curry powder, cayenne pepper, salt and pepper. Place the wings in the bowl and stir to coat. Marinate for 30 minutes.

2. Start a charcoal grill or heat a grill pan to medium high heat. Place the wings on the grill and cook until charred on the outside and an instant read thermometer reads 165 degrees F.

3. Remove wings from the grill and allow to rest 5 minutes before servings.

MASSAMAN CURRY

PREP TIME: 15 MINUTES | COOK TIME: 30 MINUTES | SERVINGS: 4

Ingredients

- 2 lbs. chicken breast, cut into chunks
- 2 tablespoons vegetable oil
- 3 Yukon Gold potatoes, cut into chunks

- 1 red onion, quartered
- 1/2 cup massaman curry paste
- 12 oz. beer
- 2 cans coconut milk
- 1 cup chicken broth

- 1 tablespoon sugar
- 1/2 teaspoon cayenne pepper
- 1/4 cup fish sauce
- Salt and black pepper

Directions

1. Season chicken with salt and pepper. Heat oil in a Dutch oven over medium heat. Add the chicken, cooking until golden brown. Remove from the pot.

2. Place potatoes in the pot and cook until browned. Remove from pot. Add the onions to the pot and cook until caramelized. Remove from the pot and store with the potatoes.

3. Add the curry paste to the pot and cook until fragrant. Add the beer, bring to a boil and reduce by half. Place the chicken, coconut milk and broth in the pot and simmer for 1-1/2 hours on low heat.

4. Return the potatoes to the pot and cook until fork tender. Remove the pot from the heat and add the fish sauce, lime juice, and cayenne pepper. Season to taste with salt and black pepper.

RED CURRY SCALLOPS

PREP TIME: 10 MINUTES | COOK TIME: 5 MINUTES | SERVINGS: 2

Ingredients

- 6 large diver scallops
- 3 tablespoons ghee
- 2 teaspoons red curry powder
- 1/2 cup plain yogurt
- 1/2 cup cucumber, shredded
- Salt and black pepper

Directions

1. Heat a skillet over medium high heat and add the ghee and curry powder. Stir well to mix ghee and curry.

2. Season the scallops with salt and black pepper.

3. Combine the yogurt and cucumber and set aside.

4. Add the scallops to the pan and cook 90 seconds per side. Serve immediately, topped with a small dollop of yogurt sauce.

CURRY TILAPIA

PREP TIME: 30 MINUTES | COOK TIME: 15 MINUTES | SERVINGS: 4

Ingredients

- 4 tilapia filets
- 1 tablespoon yellow curry powder
- 1 tablespoon olive oil
- 1 tablespoon vegetable oil
- 1 jalapeno pepper, minced
- 1 teaspoon garlic powder
- 1 mango, diced
- 1/2 red onion, chopped
- 2 tablespoons lime juice
- 1/3 cup cilantro, chopped
- Salt and black pepper

Directions

1. In a bowl, combine the olive oil, curry powder, and garlic powder. Rub the tilapia with the spice mixture and set aside.

2. In a large skillet over medium heat, add the vegetable oil and cook the fish for 3 minutes per side. Remove from pan and rest five minutes.

3. While the fish rests, combine the mango, onion, jalapeno, lime juice, and cilantro in a large bowl. Serve the fish topped with the mango salsa.

LIME CURRY CHICKEN

PREP TIME: 10 MINUTES | COOK TIME: 30 MINUTES | SERVINGS: 4

Ingredients

- 2 lbs. chicken thighs, cut into chunks
- 2 tablespoons vegetable oil
- 2 tablespoons yellow curry paste
- 2 Yukon Gold potatoes, cubed and par cooked
- Zest of 1 lime
- 2 cups coconut milk
- 2 tablespoons soy sauce
- 2 tablespoons fish sauce
- 1 red bell pepper, sliced
- Juice from 1 lime

Directions

1. In a large skillet, heat the oil and add the chicken, cooking until nearly cooked through, and set aside. In the same pan add the curry paste, and cook until very fragrant. Add the coconut milk, lime zest, potatoes, soy sauce, fish sauce, and bell pepper. Simmer for 15 minutes over low heat.

2. Add the chicken back to the pan and simmer an additional 5 minutes. Remove from heat and stir in lime juice.

CURRY CRAB SOUP

PREP TIME: 15 MINUTES | COOK TIME: 45 MINUTES | SERVINGS: 4

Ingredients

- 3/4 lb. lump crab meat
- 2 tablespoons vegetable oil
- 2 cups coconut milk
- 2 cups fish stock
- 2 tablespoons red curry paste
- 1/2 yellow onion, finely chopped
- 1/4 dry sherry
- 1 tablespoon fish sauce
- 1 stalk lemongrass

Directions

1. In a large pot over medium heat, add the oil and onions, cooking until soft. Add the sherry and cook off alcohol. Add the curry paste and lemongrass, and cook until fragrant.

2. Add the coconut milk, fish stock, and fish sauce to the pot and stir until all curry paste is dissolved. Simmer for 30 minutes.

3. Remove the lemongrass stalk from the pot and stir in the crab meat. Serve immediately.

JUNGLE CURRY WITH TOFU

PREP TIME: 5 MINUTES | COOK TIME: 20 MINUTES | SERVINGS: 4

Ingredients

- 1 (12 oz.) package extra firm tofu
- 2 tablespoons vegetable oil
- 1 red bell pepper, cut into strips
- 2 tablespoons green curry paste
- 1 cup vegetable broth
- 3 tablespoons soy sauce
- 2 teaspoons sugar
- Zest of 1 lime

Directions

1. Drain the tofu and dry with paper towels.

2. In a large skillet over medium heat, add 1 tablespoon of vegetable oil and tofu. Cook until the tofu is browned on all sides and remove from pan.

3. Add the remaining oil and bell pepper and cook until peppers become soft. Add the curry paste and cook until fragrant, then add the broth, soy sauce, sugar, and zest.
Simmer for 5 to 10 minutes and then add the tofu back to the pan. Stir to coat and serve with steamed rice.

CURRY PEANUT BRITTLE

PREP TIME: 20 MINUTES | COOK TIME: 15 MINUTES | SERVINGS: 8

Ingredients

- 3/4 cups white sugar
- 1/4 cup brown sugar
- 1/2 cup corn syrup
- 1 cup roasted peanuts
- 1 teaspoon yellow curry powder
- 1 tablespoon butter
- 1 teaspoon baking soda
- 1 teaspoon vanilla

Directions

1. Line a baking sheet with parchment paper.

2. In a microwave safe bowl, combine the sugar and corn syrup and microwave for 3 minutes, stir, and cook an additional 3 minutes. Remove from the microwave and add the peanuts and curry powder. Stir well and place back in the microwave for 2 minutes. Remove from the microwave and stir well. Add the vanilla and butter, stirring until butter is melted. Add the baking soda and stir.

3. Pour the mixture onto the parchment paper and spread thin with a spatula. Allow to cool completely before breaking into smaller pieces.

KITCHEN UNIT CONVERSION

1 teaspoon = 1/3 tbsp	=	4.9 ml
1 dessertspoon = 2 tsp	=	9.9 ml
1 tablespoon = 1.5 dstsp / 3 tsp	=	14.8 ml
1 fuid ounce = 2 tbsp / 6 tsp	=	29.6 ml
1 cup = 16 tbsp / 48 tsp	=	236.6 ml
1 quart = 4 cup	=	946 ml
1 gal = 4 quart / 16 cup	=	3.79 l
1 ounce = 2 tbsp	=	28.4 g
1 pounds = 16 oz	=	453.6 g

Printed in Great Britain
by Amazon

26366630R00044